# Who Was
# Galileo?

# Who Was Galileo?

by Patricia Brennan Demuth

illustrated by John O'Brien

Penguin Workshop

For Athena Hope Demuth, a shining star—PBD

For Linda—JO

PENGUIN WORKSHOP
An Imprint of Penguin Random House LLC, New York

The publisher does not have any control over and does not assume any responsibility for author or third-party websites or their content.

Visit us online at www.penguinrandomhouse.com.

Library of Congress Control Number: 2014045708

ISBN 9780448479859                                    10 9 8 7 6 5 4 3 2

Part of the *What Is Science & Technology?* Boxed Set, ISBN 9780593090138

# Contents

# Who Was Galileo?

AUGUST 1609. PADUA, ITALY.

It was a bright, starry night. A scientist named Galileo walked outside to his back garden. He carried a new telescope that he'd made himself. For weeks, Galileo had been carefully grinding the lenses. Now his telescope could enlarge objects many times their size.

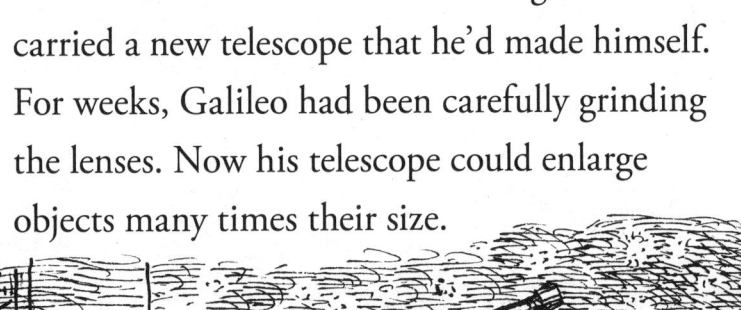

Galileo pointed the telescope upward. Dazzling
sights leaped into view—sights no one had ever
seen. How could they? These sights were not
visible to the naked eye. Over the next few weeks,

Galileo roamed the heavens with his telescope.
What he saw amazed him. Mountains rose up
from the moon's surface! New stars took form from
fuzzy patches in the sky! Moons circled Jupiter!

Yet Galileo's discoveries led him into trouble. Terrible trouble. What he saw convinced him that the sun was the center of the universe—not the Earth. In 1609 this was a strange idea. For thousands of years, people thought that the sun and all the planets circled Earth once a day. The Catholic church held this belief as well.

When Galileo lived, the church was very powerful in Italy. It had its own court, called the Inquisition. The Inquisition could arrest and try heretics—anyone who spoke against the church's teachings. Heretics were sometimes tortured, even killed.

Galileo was torn. He himself was a faithful Catholic who honored church teachings. Yet his own eyes pointed him to a different truth.

This truth would put his life at stake.

# Chapter 1
# Boyhood

On February 15, 1564, Galileo was born in Pisa, Italy. His full name had a musical ring: Galileo Galilei (gal-uh-LAY-oh gal-uh-LAY). Yet the great scientist became known by just his first name. Italy honored its most famous citizens that way, including the painter Michelangelo. Even books by Galileo were printed without his last name. And today, encyclopedias list him simply as *Galileo*.

He was born into an exciting age known as the Renaissance. Discovery was in the air. Europe was exploding with a renewed interest in the arts and science. In 1564 the English writer William Shakespeare was born, and Michelangelo died. Both men, along with Galileo, went down in history as geniuses of the Renaissance.

WILLIAM SHAKESPEARE  MICHELANGELO

The printing press, invented in 1454, allowed books to be mass-produced instead of being copied by hand, one by one. With more books, more people began to read.

# THE RENAISSANCE

IN ANCIENT TIMES, GREECE AND ROME FOSTERED THE ARTS, SCIENCE, AND PHILOSOPHY. BUT AFTER THE FALL OF ROME AROUND 500 AD, ADVANCES IN EUROPE SLOWED TO A CRAWL. THE PERIOD BECAME KNOWN AS THE DARK AGES.

THEN, HUNDREDS OF YEARS LATER, CAME THE

RENAISSANCE. *RENAISSANCE* COMES FROM A FRENCH WORD MEANING "REBIRTH." IT WAS A CULTURAL MOVEMENT THAT STARTED IN ITALY ABOUT 1300, SPREAD THROUGH EUROPE, AND LASTED ABOUT THREE HUNDRED YEARS. LEARNING AND THE ARTS TOOK GREAT LEAPS FORWARD. ARTISTS AND PHILOSOPHERS LOOKED TO ANCIENT GREECE AND ROME FOR INSPIRATION.

DAVID BY MICHELANGELO

Artists such as Michelangelo and Leonardo da Vinci created beautiful paintings, sculpture, and architecture. With improved seagoing instruments, explorers bravely set sail for uncharted lands.

MONA LISA

Christopher Columbus arrived in the New World of the Americas in 1492. Ferdinand Magellan's crew sailed around the globe, returning in 1522.

And in 1607, when Galileo was forty-three, settlers arrived in Jamestown and founded one of the first English settlements in North America.

Pisa was a beautiful old city by the River Arno. Its cathedral was already five centuries old when Galileo was born. Pisa's most famous landmark stood—or rather, *tilted*—beside the cathedral. It was called the Leaning Tower because it looked ready to topple at any moment.

LEANING TOWER

# THE LEANING TOWER OF PISA

IN 1178 WORKERS STARTED TO BUILD A BELL TOWER BEHIND THE CATHEDRAL OF PISA. UNFORTUNATELY, THE TOWER WAS BUILT ON SOFT, SANDY SOIL THAT COULDN'T HOLD UP THE TOWER'S WEIGHT. EVEN BEFORE THE TOWER WAS FINISHED, IT BEGAN LEANING HEAVILY TO ONE SIDE. TODAY PISA IS KNOWN WORLDWIDE FOR ITS LEANING TOWER.

Galileo was the firstborn child. His mother and father both came from noble Italian families. However, that didn't mean the couple was wealthy. Galileo's father, Vincenzio, worked hard as a musician. He sang, played the lute, wrote songs, and taught.

Vincenzio also wrote books about music theory. His books stirred up trouble. Songwriters were supposed to follow strict rules for composing. But Vincenzio questioned the rules. He even added notes to the scale!

Old masters tried to stop one of his books from being published. Vincenzio, however, was able to push it into print. "I . . . wish to be allowed freely to question . . . in search of truth," he said. Young Galileo listened carefully. Years later, he would be bold and outspoken, too.

Even as a boy, Galileo was gifted. His curiosity had no limits. He took apart machines to see how they worked. And he invented clever little toys and moving gadgets of his own.

Galileo also spent hours and hours learning music and drawing. His father taught him to play the lute. This stringed instrument was as popular then as guitars are now. Playing the lute became a lifelong passion for Galileo. From tutors, he learned to draw in perspective, which meant things looked as if they were in three-dimensional space. He practiced drawing objects and scenes until they looked perfectly lifelike. Years later, Galileo's art skills would come in very handy.

When Galileo was eight, his family moved to Florence. Vincenzio had a wonderful new job playing music at the royal court. Galileo remained in Pisa to study with tutors, and then he joined the rest of his family.

Florence was a thrilling place to live. During the Renaissance, the city was a center for learning and the arts. It was the capital city of an area called Tuscany. Vincenzio's job at the palace let the family mingle with dukes and princes.

At age eleven, Galileo was sent to a monastery to begin school. There the Catholic monks taught him everything an educated person of the 1500s needed to know. Galileo learned the Greek and Latin languages. And he studied the ancient subject of logic, learning how to break down and solve complex problems in an orderly way.

Galileo also studied religion. It interested him so much that he decided to become a monk. The idea horrified his father. As the oldest son, Galileo was expected to support his family one day. A poor monk couldn't do that. Vincenzio quickly withdrew Galileo from the monastery. After that, Galileo lived at home and studied at a nearby school.

At seventeen, Galileo was ready for university. Back then, very few young men had the chance to attend one. Only the sons of rich or noble families could usually afford to go. (Girls were not allowed to enter.) But Vincenzio was determined to give his smart son the best education possible.

# Chapter 2
# Hungry for Knowledge

In 1581 Galileo enrolled at the University of Pisa, back in his hometown. Doctors were well paid and respected. So Galileo's father wanted him to study medicine.

Soon Galileo stood out at the university.
It wasn't just because of his reddish hair and
curly beard. Galileo liked to argue about ideas.

Even though he was eager to learn, he questioned
everything. His classmates nicknamed Galileo
"the Wrangler."

Some teachers disliked Galileo. They weren't used to being questioned. But many teachers and students enjoyed his sharp wit. As a friend, Galileo was warm, loyal, and very generous. For his whole life, people would react strongly to Galileo. He made strong friends . . . and strong enemies.

One day Galileo heard a lecture that set his mind afire. He realized that nature ran with perfect order, ruled by unseen laws. These laws were written in a special code: mathematics. "The Universe cannot be read until we have learned the language in which it is written," Galileo wrote later. "It is written in mathematical language. And the letters are triangles, circles, and other geometrical figures."

Galileo poured himself into the study of math. He puzzled over things that other people didn't even notice. At the cathedral one day, Galileo looked up at a huge lamp hanging on a chain from the ceiling. A repairman had just let go of the chain. Now it was swinging in the air.

Galileo saw that it seemed to be swinging with a regular rhythm. He timed the swings using his pulse. The swings got shorter and shorter. But, sure enough, every full swing, back and forth, took the same amount of time.

In his room, Galileo tested his idea. He wanted to be certain it was right. It was—every single time. A pendulum swinging wide and fast takes the same amount of time to go back and forth as when it slows nearly to a stop. Only making the chain longer or shorter will change the timing. At age nineteen, Galileo had discovered a mathematical law. It is now called the law of the pendulum.

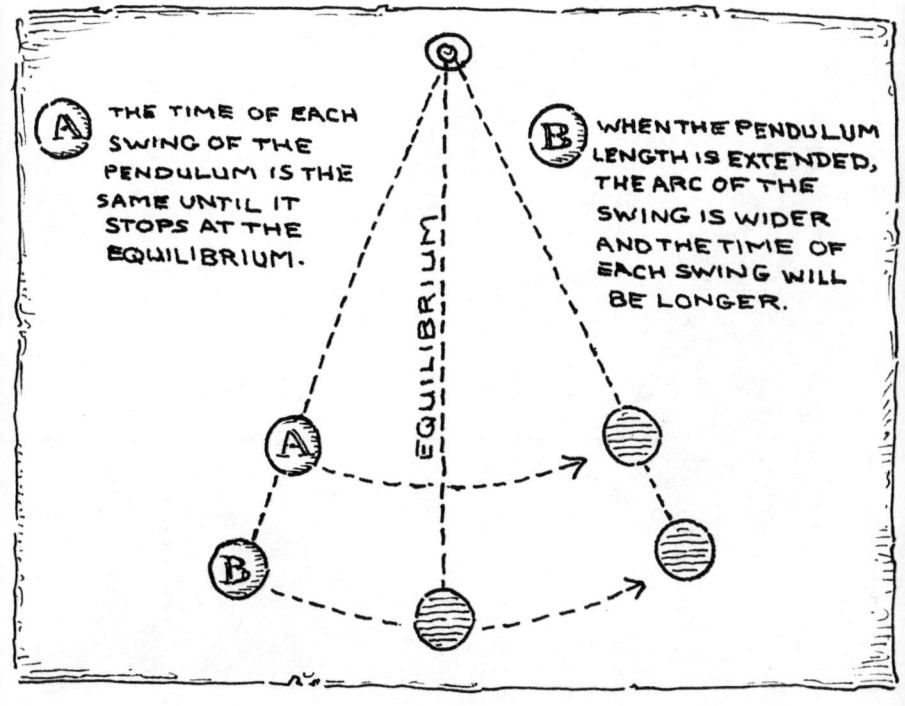

(A) THE TIME OF EACH SWING OF THE PENDULUM IS THE SAME UNTIL IT STOPS AT THE EQUILIBRIUM.

(B) WHEN THE PENDULUM LENGTH IS EXTENDED, THE ARC OF THE SWING IS WIDER AND THE TIME OF EACH SWING WILL BE LONGER.

EQUILIBRIUM

Today, scientists always do experiments to test out their ideas—but not in Galileo's time. He was the first scientist to use this approach, called the scientific method. It's one reason that Galileo is known as the father of modern science.

His interest in math made Galileo fall behind in his medical classes. He had no passion for medicine, anyway. In 1585, after four years in Pisa, Galileo left the university without any degree.

Returning home, Galileo taught students privately in math and gave public lectures.

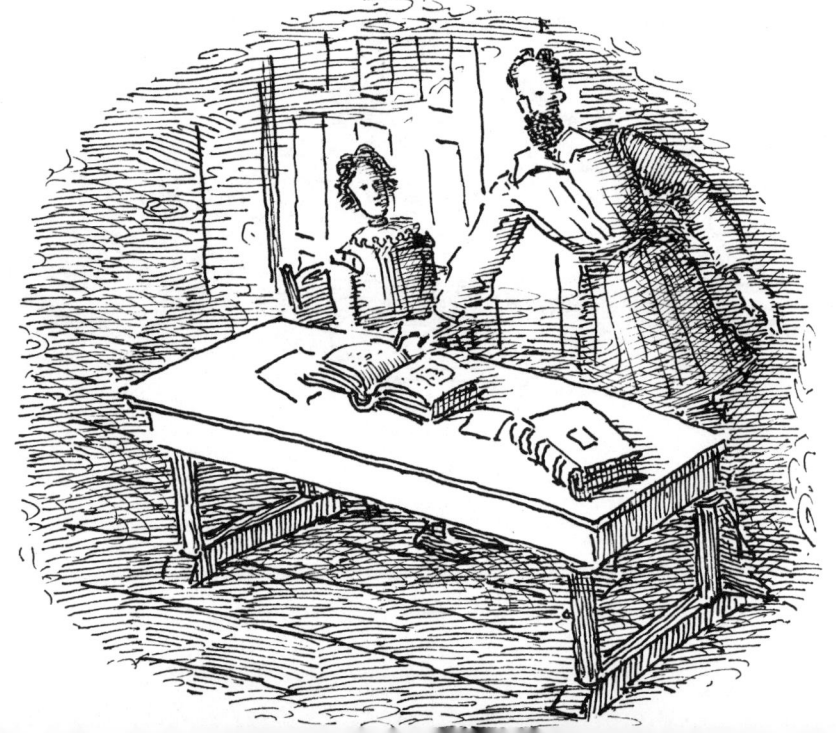

He also kept doing his own research. As Galileo uncovered new truths about nature, he looked for ways to put them to use. Galileo took up inventing again, just as he had done as a child.

For months he studied the nature of water, posing questions to himself. What was the energy on top of water that made things float? At what point did waterfalls break? His research led him to invent a pump. It helped farmers take water from a river to irrigate their crops.

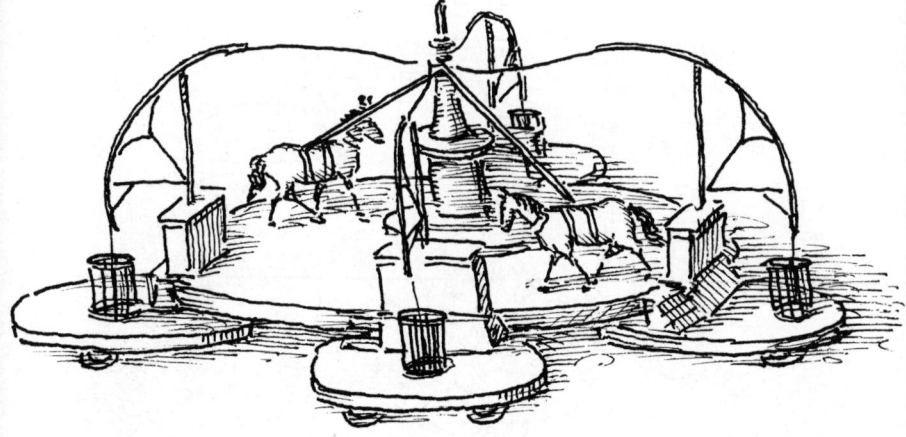

Next, he invented a new balance, or scale. One side of the balance was in water, the other in air. Jewelers loved the balance. It showed them exactly how much silver or

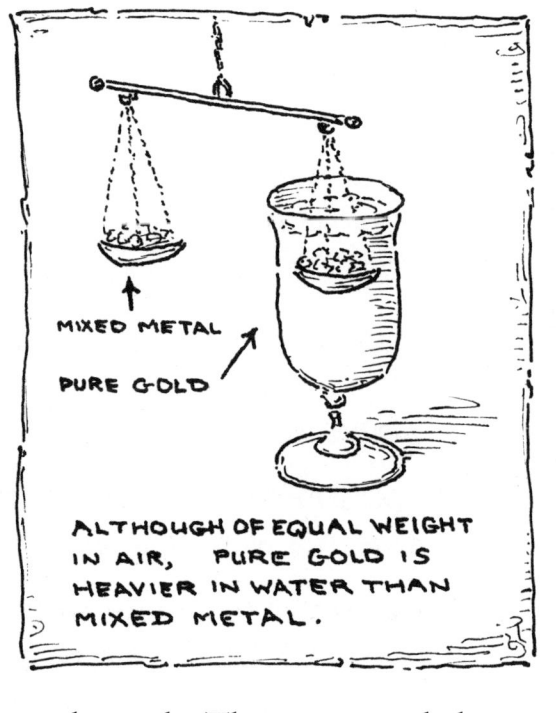

MIXED METAL

PURE GOLD

ALTHOUGH OF EQUAL WEIGHT IN AIR, PURE GOLD IS HEAVIER IN WATER THAN MIXED METAL.

gold was inside mixed metals. The invention led Galileo to write his first book, *The Little Balance*.

Word of his outstanding work spread throughout Italy. In 1589 the University of Pisa offered Galileo a job teaching mathematics. What an opportunity! Four years earlier he had dropped out of the university without a degree. Now he returned as a professor.

# TEST THE PENDULUM YOURSELF

GALILEO WROTE THE LAW OF THE PENDULUM IN A FORMULA THAT IS HARD TO UNDERSTAND UNLESS YOU ARE A MATHEMATICIAN. HOWEVER, IT'S NOT HARD TO DO HIS BASIC TEST ON YOUR OWN.

- MAKE A SIMPLE PENDULUM WITH A PIECE OF STRING AND A WEIGHT. (A FISHING WEIGHT WORKS WELL.)

- HOLDING THE END OF THE STRING LIGHTLY, GIVE THE WEIGHT A PUSH.

- WATCH THE PENDULUM SWING FREELY FROM POINT A TO POINT B (SEE ILLUSTRATION). CAN YOU NOTICE THE EVEN TIMING, EVEN AS THE PENDULUM SLOWS DOWN?

- CUT THE STRING AND REPEAT THE EXPERIMENT. THE SWINGS ARE SLOWER, RIGHT?

A     B

# Chapter 3
## A Rebel Teacher

The new teacher at the University of Pisa was causing a stir. He refused to wear the proper robes of a professor! It was supposed to be an honor to wear the long black togas. But Galileo thought they were silly and a nuisance. He mocked the robes in a long, funny poem. University officials weren't laughing, though. They docked Galileo's pay!

The University of Pisa based its teaching on the works of Aristotle (eh-ruh-STOT-ull). So did most universities throughout Europe. Aristotle was an ancient Greek philosopher who

ARISTOTLE

had lived from 384 BC to 322 BC. His books covered a wide range of topics—including science and math. He seemed to have answers for every question about the universe. Galileo had to teach Aristotle's ideas in his classroom. But, in his own mind, he dared to question some of Aristotle's teachings.

For example, Aristotle said that heavy objects fall faster than light ones. For almost two thousand years, no one had ever doubted this. It seemed to make sense that a hammer would fall faster than a feather. But Galileo had noticed hailstones of varying sizes hit the ground at the same time. All objects fall at the same speed, he decided.

Other scholars scoffed at this notion. Who was Galileo to question Aristotle, anyway?

According to a famous story, Galileo decided to put his theory to the test. He led a group of professors to the top of the Leaning Tower of Pisa. He brought along a ten-pound cannonball and a one-pound lead ball. According to Aristotle, the cannonball should fall to the ground ten times faster than the lighter ball. On a signal, the balls were both dropped from the tower. Both balls thudded to the ground at almost exactly the same moment. (Air slowed down the lighter ball just a bit.)

It seemed that Galileo had proved his point.
But some observers thought Galileo had proved
only one thing: He was a troublemaker. Galileo's
students, however, liked their entertaining teacher.
Most of his classes had standing room only.
Sometimes professors came to his classes, too.
But they came to hiss and boo.

# PROVING GALILEO RIGHT

IN 1972 TWO *APOLLO 15* ASTRONAUTS, DAVID
SCOTT AND JIM IRWIN, LANDED ON THE MOON.
UNLIKE EARTH, THE MOON HAS NO AIR RESISTANCE.
SCOTT DROPPED A HAMMER AND A FEATHER TO
SEE WHICH ONE WOULD FALL FASTER. EACH ONE
HIT THE MOON AT EXACTLY THE SAME TIME.

THIS WAS JUST WHAT GALILEO HAD PREDICTED 370 YEARS EARLIER. ASTRONAUT SCOTT RADIOED TO NASA, "THIS PROVES THAT MR. GALILEO WAS CORRECT."

THE MOON TEST WAS BROADCAST LIVE ON TV. YOU CAN WATCH IT ONLINE AT HTTP://ER.JSC.NASA. GOV/SEH/FEATHER.HTML.

In 1591 Galileo's three-year contract at the university was almost up. Knowing he was likely to lose his job, Galileo resigned.

It was an awful time to be jobless. Galileo's father had died recently. Now his mother, two younger sisters, and a brother needed him to support them. Where could he find work to take care of his family?

Luckily, a new job came before too long. The University of Padua hired Galileo to teach mathematics. The pay there was better than at Pisa.

UNIVERSITY OF PADUA

Plus, the University of Padua was a freethinking place. It was a perfect fit for the independent and brilliant thinker.

Galileo was so poor when he set off for Padua that he could not afford to ride by horse. He walked the whole way—one hundred miles!

# Chapter 4
## Happy Years

In old age, Galileo looked back on the time he spent at Padua as the happiest years of his life. He was twenty-eight when he arrived. Soon after, the University of Padua promoted Galileo to be head of the math department. The post was his for the next eighteen years.

Young noblemen from all over Europe flocked
to the university to study. When they returned
home, they brought word of Galileo and his ideas.
Galileo's reputation grew and grew. In Padua, he
also attracted a lively circle of friends. They were
the greatest minds of their time.

The city of Venice was nearby. Galileo often
rode the ferry there to spend the holidays.
Venice was a charming city of canals. People got
around by riding boats. The city's palaces housed
beautiful works of art.

# ITALY IN GALILEO'S TIME

IN THE 1500S, ITALY WASN'T A SINGLE COUNTRY AS IT IS TODAY. IT WAS A GROUP OF CITY-STATES. EACH CITY-STATE WAS MADE UP OF A CAPITAL CITY AND SMALLER VILLAGES. EACH STATE HAD ITS OWN RULER AND GOVERNMENT.

ITALY'S THREE MOST IMPORTANT CAPITAL CITIES WERE VENICE, FLORENCE, AND ROME. VENICE WAS A WEALTHY SHIPPING CITY IN NORTHEAST ITALY. ROME WAS THE CAPITAL OF THE POWERFUL PAPAL STATES, RULED BY THE POPE, HEAD OF THE CATHOLIC CHURCH. FLORENCE FLOWERED DURING THE RENAISSANCE AS A CENTER OF THE ARTS. MICHELANGELO AND LEONARDO DA VINCI BOTH CAME FROM THERE.

In Venice, Galileo fell in love with Marina Gamba. Because she was from a lower social class, it was difficult for Galileo to marry her. Also, professors were expected to stay single and devote themselves to their work. Nonetheless, Galileo and Marina developed a long relationship and had children together. A daughter, Virginia, was born in 1600. One year later, a second daughter, Livia, followed. A son, named Vincenzio after Galileo's father, was born in 1606.

Galileo provided generously for his children and Marina. He moved them to a house that was five minutes away so he could spend more time with his family. Later Marina married another man, but that was after Galileo had moved away from Padua. All her life, she stayed strong friends with Galileo.

Although Galileo loved the years in Padua, he nearly died there. One hot afternoon, Galileo and two friends decided to take their afternoon nap in an underground room. A cool breeze was piped into the room from a nearby mountain cave.

Somehow, a poisonous gas from the cave slipped through the pipes! The three men fell terribly ill. The next day, one of the friends died. The second died a few days later. Galileo pulled through. However, bad health troubled him for the rest of his life, sometimes keeping him in bed for weeks at a time.

Galileo now had two families to support, so money was often tight. In those days, a bride's family paid the groom wedding money, known as a dowry. The dowry for Galileo's sister cost as much as his yearly salary! Fortunately, more money came in from a couple of Galileo's inventions.

In 1597 Galileo invented a handheld instrument called the geometric and military compass.

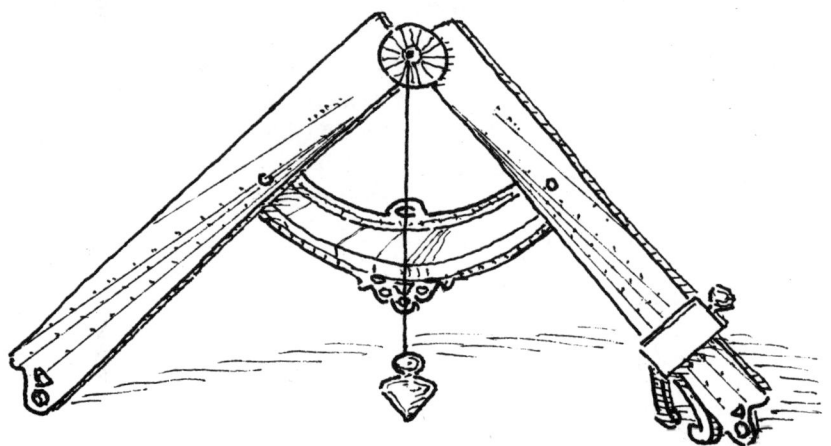

The compass looked like two metal rulers covered with numbers. With a simple slide of the compass, people were able to solve all kinds of hard math problems. Bankers used the compass to figure the exchange rates for all the different monies used in European countries. Shipbuilders used it to test scale models of new designs before building a full-size ship. Generals at war used it to arrange armies on the battlefield and to set the correct charge for any size of cannon.

Next, Galileo invented an early thermometer. Now, for the first time, people could measure the temperature of air. The thermometer (called a thermoscope) worked by drawing water up a heated glass tube. The higher the temperature of the tube, the higher the water rose in it. Common thermometers

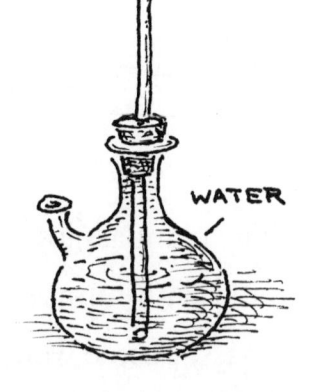

— AIR

WATER
EXPANDS UP
THE TUBE
AS IT
WARMS UP

WATER

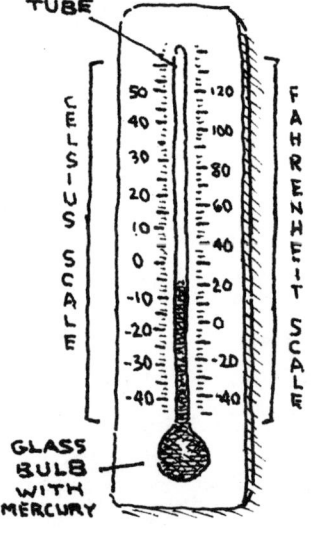

EXPANSION TUBE

CELSIUS SCALE

FAHRENHEIT SCALE

GLASS BULB WITH MERCURY

of today still work in a similar way—with heat drawing liquid up a tube.

Galileo also continued doing important research in the field of physics (the science that studies energy). Falling objects were on his mind again. He knew that all objects sped up as they fell. But by how much exactly? Galileo was determined to find out the mathematical rule.

Falling through air happened in the blink of an eye. It was way too fast for anyone to time. So Galileo first had to find a way to slow down a fall. He did it by building a slope out of a board. At equal spaces across the board, he laid strings that had bells attached. Then Galileo rolled a metal ball down the slope. The bells rang as the ball passed, allowing Galileo to time how fast the ball fell in a measured distance.

After hours of testing,
Galileo uncovered a nifty rule
of motion. Falling balls gathered speed at the
rates of one, three, five, and seven. Galileo called
it the odd-numbers rule. Galileo tested the rule
again and again, by adjusting the slope to make it
steeper. The odd-numbers rule held firm each and
every time.

In 1609 interesting news reached Galileo. A
spyglass had been invented that made faraway
things appear closer. Galileo didn't know it then,
but the little spyglass would change his life.

# THINKING IN NUMBERS

AS GALILEO DID HIS EXPERIMENTS ON MOTION, HE SCRIBBLED DOWN COMPLEX NUMBERS, EQUATIONS, AND GRAPHS. COPIES OF HIS NOTES WERE PRESERVED. THEY GIVE US A GLIMPSE INSIDE THE MIND OF A HARDWORKING GENIUS. CLEARLY, GALILEO THOUGHT IN NUMBERS, NOT IN WORDS.

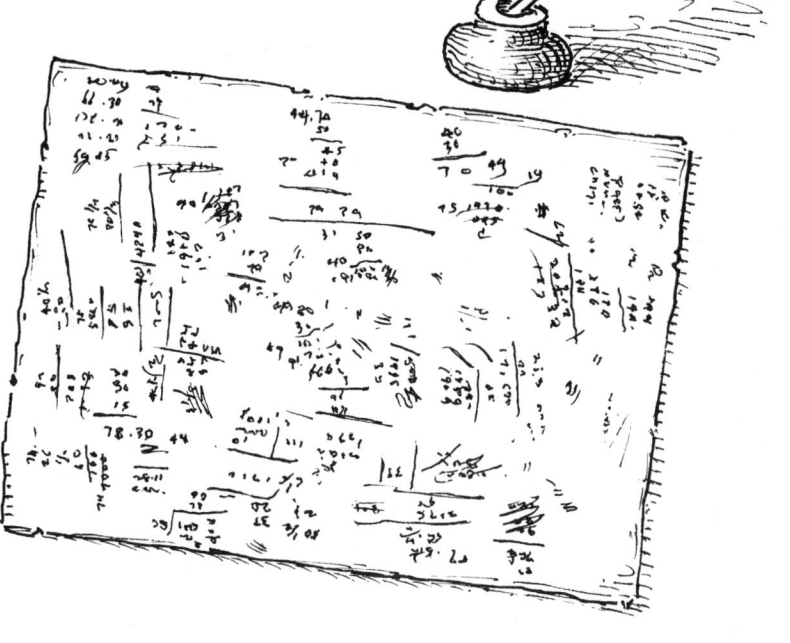

# Chapter 5
## Looking at the Heavens

Eyeglasses had been around since the 1200s.
But until 1608, no one used glass lenses to magnify
far-off objects so they could be seen. Then a Dutch
lens maker named Hans Lippershey put two lenses
inside a tube. One lens curved outward (convex);

HANS LIPPERSHEY

one curved inward (concave). The tube, named a spyglass, enlarged things four times their normal size.

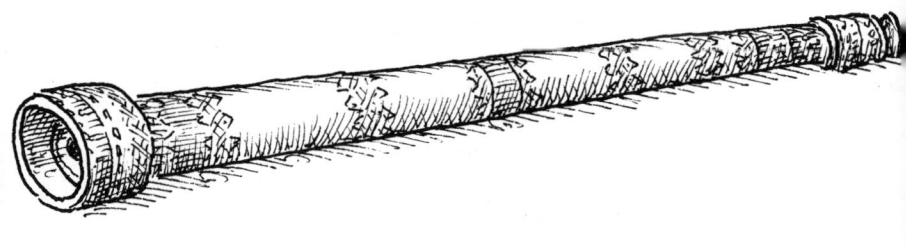

The spyglass was sold as a toy. But Galileo immediately saw its greater importance. The navy in Venice could use it to spot enemy ships from afar! Venice, a port city, had the biggest navy in Europe. Now it would be the best.

Galileo set to work making his own spyglass. First he had to teach himself to grind and polish lenses. It was painstaking work. In a few days, he had made a spyglass as good as Lippershey's. Not long after, he made one much better. It could magnify objects tenfold. Galileo had taken a toy and turned it into an instrument of science.

People soon renamed it the telescope. (The prefix *tele-* means "far off.")

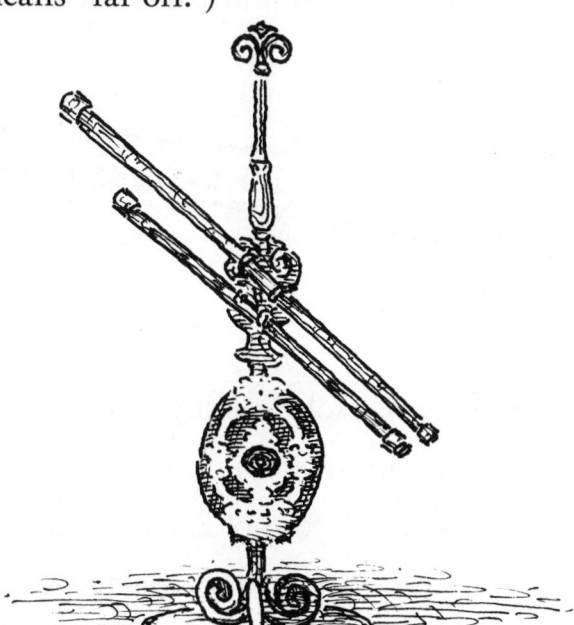

## GALILEO'S TELESCOPES

Galileo hurried off to Venice to show his telescope to the senators who governed the city. They took turns looking out to sea. To their amazement, they spotted ships two or three hours before onlookers on shore could see them! Galileo gave them his telescope free of charge.

They rewarded Galileo with a pay raise and a lifetime contract at the University of Padua.

Back home, Galileo continued to improve the telescope, reshaping pieces of glass again and again. By the time he was satisfied, he had an instrument that was twenty to thirty times more powerful than the human eye.

It was time to turn his telescope toward the heavens.

One night in late November 1609, Galileo pointed the telescope at the huge fuzzy patch in the sky known as the Milky Way. Out of the darkness shone an extraordinary number of stars, packed closely together. As Galileo continued stargazing on other nights, he found eighty new stars in the constellation Orion. Before this, only nine stars in Orion had been identified.

Galileo stood in awe of the heavenly sights. "It has pleased God to make me alone the [witness] to an admirable thing kept hidden all these ages," he wrote.

Next, Galileo studied the moon. Everyone at the time thought that the moon was perfectly smooth. After all, that was what Aristotle had claimed. Galileo's telescope, however, revealed something far different. The surface of the moon was rough, like Earth's. Mountains, valleys, and craters filled its landscape. Using his math skills, Galileo even measured how high the lunar mountains stood.

Every night, Galileo drew detailed sketches
of what he had seen. His pictures captured the
changing shadows on the face of the moon as it
passed through its phases.

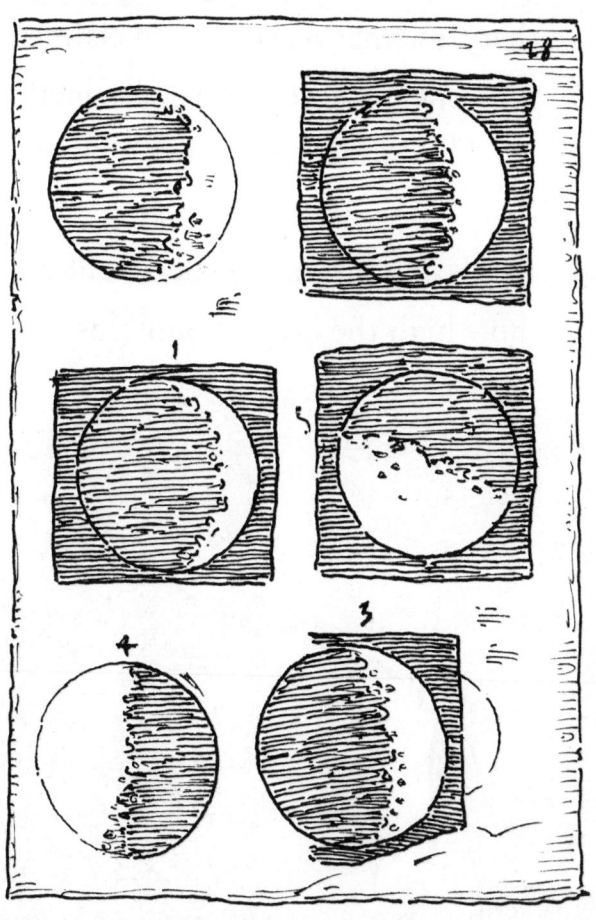

GALILEO'S DRAWING

Just one month later, Galileo made his greatest discovery in astronomy. On a clear night in January 1610, he aimed the telescope at Jupiter. What were those three bright bodies hovering near the planet? Were they stars? The next night, he saw that the three bodies had *moved*! That proved they couldn't be stars, which always appeared in the same places in the heavens. In less than a week, a fourth body appeared on Jupiter's other side. Galileo soon realized that all four bodies were orbiting the planet, just like our moon orbits Earth! He had discovered four moons of Jupiter! No one had found anything new in the solar system for over fifteen hundred years.

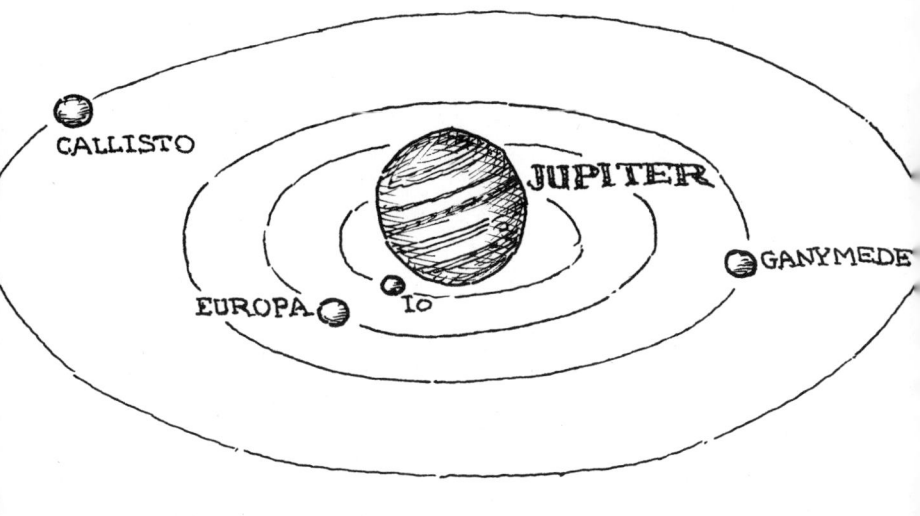

In the short span of eight weeks, Galileo uncovered an astounding number of heavenly secrets. They still stand as the most amazing series of discoveries ever made by a single astronomer.

# Chapter 6
# The Starry Messenger

Galileo set to work writing a book about his discoveries. His drawings of the stars and moon became the illustrations. The book was entitled *The Starry Messenger.* The title referred to Galileo's new telescope. But it described Galileo himself just as well.

Galileo wrote *The Starry Messenger* in Latin. It was the written language used by learned men all over Europe. That way, people in countries outside Italy could read it, too. The book became an immediate best seller all over Europe. It made Galileo very famous.

Galileo hoped the book would also attract a wealthy patron—such as the Medici family. Finding a good patron was important to

Renaissance scholars. Patrons gave them money to support their work. The Medicis were not only the rulers of Tuscany. They were also known to be very generous patrons.

GRAND DUKE COSIMO II

So Galileo dedicated *The Starry Messenger* to Grand Duke Cosimo II. He was head of the Medicis in Italy. Galileo presented the book to the grand duke along with the telescope he'd used to search the heavens. And Galileo didn't stop there. He named the four Jupiter moons the Medicean Stars, after the four Medici brothers. (Today, the moons of Jupiter have different names—Io, Europa, Ganymede, and Callisto.)

Galileo's flattery paid off. The grand duke appointed him chief mathematician and philosopher of the royal court. Galileo no longer had to teach. He was free to devote all his time to research.

Soon, Galileo left Padua and moved back to his beloved Florence. Meanwhile, his book was causing an uproar. Once again, his ideas opposed Aristotle's.

Backers of Aristotle went on the attack. They said Galileo was a fraud who would do anything for attention. Some claimed that his telescope made things appear that weren't there.

Galileo grew impatient with these scholars. He thought they were stuck in their ways. "They wish never to raise their eyes from [Aristotle's] pages," he said. "As if this great book of the universe had been written to be read by nobody but Aristotle."

Galileo couldn't see why an ancient Greek philosopher should have the last word on everything. In fact, he thought that Aristotle would agree with *him* if he looked through the telescope.

# THE MEDICI FAMILY

STARTING ABOUT 1420, THE MEDICIS AMASSED A HUGE FORTUNE IN TRADE AND BANKING. WITH WEALTH CAME POWER. IN TIME, THE MEDICI FAMILY LINE INCLUDED PRINCES, DUKES, FOUR POPES, AND QUEENS OF SPAIN AND FRANCE.

MEDICIS RULED FLORENCE, ALMOST WITHOUT STOP, FROM THE 1420S TO THE 1730S. THEIR GENEROUS DONATIONS TO THE ARTS AND LEARNING HELPED MAKE FLORENCE THE CHIEF CENTER OF THE RENAISSANCE. THEIR PALACE LIBRARY WAS THE LARGEST LIBRARY IN EUROPE.

GALILEO'S CLOSE TIES TO THE MEDICIS WENT FAR BACK. HIS FATHER HAD WORKED AS ONE OF THEIR COURT MUSICIANS. GRAND DUKE COSIMO I APPOINTED GALILEO TO TEACH AT THE UNIVERSITY OF PISA IN 1589. AND GRAND DUKE COSIMO II, HIS FORMER PUPIL, BECAME HIS PATRON IN 1610.

Soon Galileo came up with an idea that would raise the biggest outcry yet. The astronomer pointed his telescope at the planet Venus. Over several nights, he watched Venus go through phases, just like our moon. Its glow changed from a sliver of light, to a half orb, to a full orb. Only one thing could explain these phases, Galileo decided. Venus must be orbiting the sun and reflecting its light.

If the planet Venus was orbiting the sun, then so was the Earth!

This idea flew in the face of commonly held beliefs. Nearly everyone agreed with Aristotle: the Earth stood absolutely still in the center of the universe. And the sun, stars, and planets circled the Earth once a day.

Galileo, however, believed in what he saw. He was sure that an earlier scientist, named Nicolaus Copernicus, had the right idea. In 1543, Copernicus had suggested that the sun was the center of the universe; the planets, including Earth, circled about it.

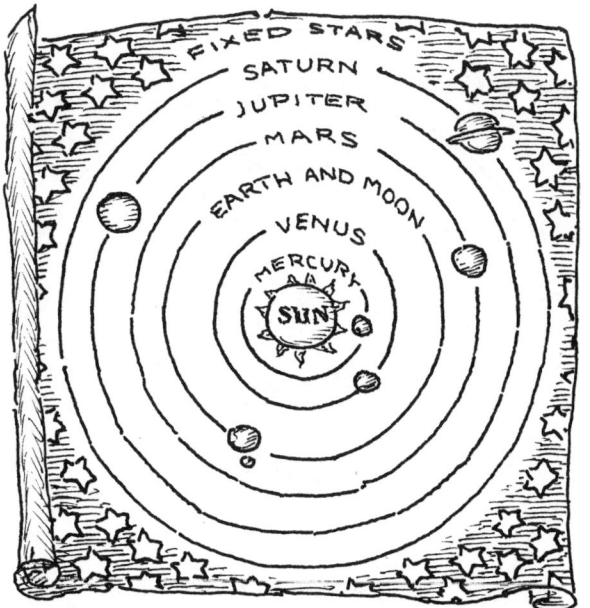

It was understandable why this idea seemed ridiculous. Every day people watched the sun moving across the sky, bringing light at sunrise and darkness at sunset. But Galileo—and Copernicus—explained night and day in another way. They suggested that the Earth spun around daily on an axis. Where the Earth faced the sun, there was daylight; where it faced away, there was night.

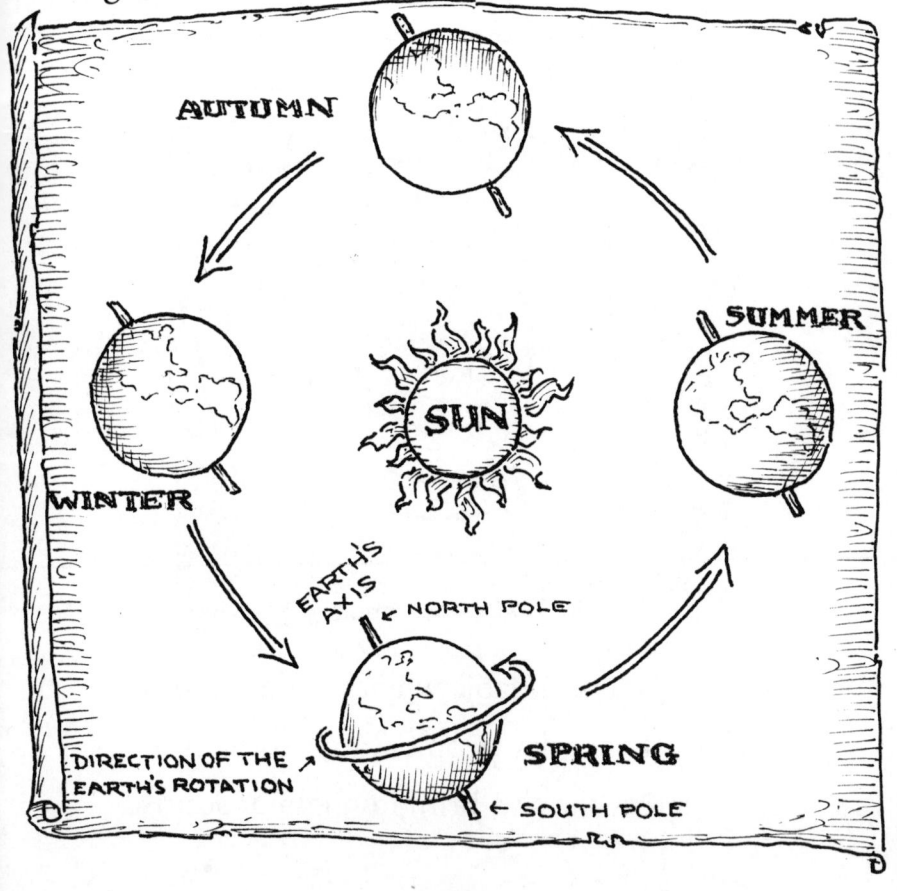

# NICOLAUS COPERNICUS

NICOLAUS COPERNICUS (1473-1543) WAS A RENAISSANCE MATHEMATICIAN AND ASTRONOMER FROM POLAND. HE WAS THE FIRST TO SUGGEST THAT THE SUN WAS THE CENTER OF THE UNIVERSE. HIS THEORY STRONGLY CONTRADICTED THE TEACHINGS AT THE TIME. HOW THEN DID COPERNICUS ESCAPE GETTING INTO THE DEEP TROUBLE THAT BEFELL GALILEO LATER ON? BY NOT ALLOWING HIS IDEA TO BE PUBLISHED UNTIL 1543, WHEN HE LAY ON HIS DEATHBED! COPERNICUS WROTE, "THE SCORN WHICH I HAD TO FEAR ON ACCOUNT OF THE NEWNESS AND ABSURDITY OF MY OPINION ALMOST DROVE ME TO ABANDON A WORK ALREADY UNDERTAKEN."

Criticism of Galileo became very heated. So, in 1611, Galileo decided to travel to Rome and defend his discoveries. He brought along his telescope so others could see what he saw.

The trip to Rome was a triumph! An important group of scientists invited Galileo to become a member. The group was made up of famous scientists from different countries. They shared their latest findings with one another. From then on, Galileo enjoyed a lively exchange of letters with his new friends.

More important, the Catholic church approved Galileo's discoveries in the heavens. Of course, that did not mean they went along with all of his conclusions. Not by any means!

# Chapter 7
# "A Very Dangerous Thing"

The attacks against Galileo did not stop. They only grew worse. Galileo continued to make findings that clashed with old ideas. He said (correctly) there were dark spots on the sun, called sunspots.

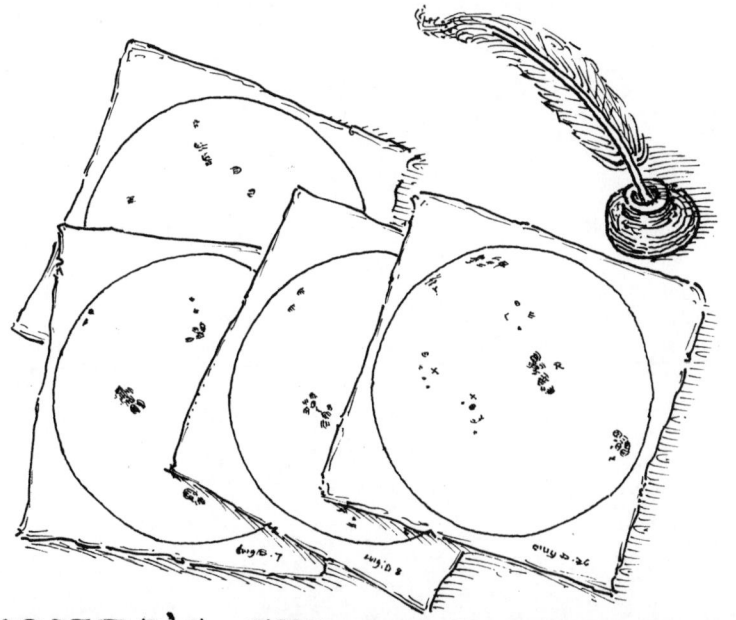

GALILEO'S SUNSPOT DRAWINGS

And bodies in water either floated or sank because of density, not size. (Correct again.) But what kept upsetting people the most was his idea that Earth did not stand at the center of the universe.

Several scientists wrote books blasting Galileo and his ideas. Galileo fought back. His tongue could be as sharp as his wit. He often treated his enemies like dimwits. "Your ignorance astounds me," he wrote to one.

A loyal circle of fellow scientists supported Galileo. They nicknamed their opponents the "Pigeon League"—in a word, birdbrains!

As the scientists warred, Galileo turned his attention to an important family matter. In 1613 he decided to place his two daughters in a convent. Virginia, age thirteen, and Livia, age twelve, would stay in the convent for the rest of their lives. Both girls became nuns when they turned sixteen. Virginia took the name Maria

Celeste. *Celeste* means "heavens." It may have been her way of honoring the astronomy of her beloved father.

In time, Galileo's enemies started to aim a new weapon at him: the Catholic church. They claimed that the sun-centered viewpoint went against the Bible. It was heresy!

Dragging religion into the fight dismayed Galileo. He was a devout Catholic with no desire whatsoever to fight the church. He felt that the charge of heresy was "worse than death."

Galileo believed firmly that the church and science held separate roles. He liked to quote a late Catholic cardinal: "The Bible was a book about how one goes to Heaven—not how Heaven goes."

Galileo wrote a forty-page letter addressed to the grand duchess of the Medici family. In it he laid out his ideas about science and religion. "Holy Scripture cannot err," he said. But its "interpreters are liable to err in many ways."

GRAND DUCHESS OF THE MEDICI FAMILY

The letter was passed from one person to another. At last it reached the hands of the Inquisition in Rome. The Inquisition ruled the letter innocent. Nonetheless, Galileo feared that his church was listening to fools. And what if the church turned against him?

In 1616 he decided to travel to Rome again. By laying out the facts, Galileo was certain he could convince the church of the rightness of his views. He was determined to stand up for his beliefs.

# SISTER MARIA CELESTE

SISTER MARIA CELESTE, GALILEO'S OLDER DAUGHTER, WAS DEVOTED TO HER FATHER. WITH A KEEN INTELLECT OF HER OWN, SHE WAS ABLE TO UNDERSTAND AND ADMIRE HIS WORK.

CONVENT LIFE WAS DEMANDING. NUNS TOOK VOWS TO NEVER MARRY AND TO OWN NOTHING. YET A GREAT MANY WOMEN OF THE TIME CHOSE THE CONVENT. THERE THEY RECEIVED AN EDUCATION AS WELL AS THE RESPECT OF CATHOLICS.

LIKE ALL NUNS, MARIA CELESTE SPENT HER DAYS IN PRAYER, HARD WORK, SACRIFICE, AND STUDY. SHE NEVER WENT OUTSIDE THE CONVENT WALLS. MUSICAL LIKE HER GRANDFATHER, SHE DIRECTED THE CHOIR AND PLAYED THE ORGAN.

IN 1617 GALILEO MOVED TO ARCETRI, JUST A FIVE-MINUTE WALK AWAY. HE OFTEN BROUGHT THE NUNS VEGETABLES FROM HIS GARDEN AND PAID THEIR BILLS. LIKEWISE, MARIA CELESTE TENDED TO HER FATHER'S NEEDS, MENDING HIS SHIRTS AND WRITING UP HIS TEXTS. THE TWO FREQUENTLY WROTE EACH OTHER LETTERS. TODAY, 120 LETTERS FROM MARIA CELESTE TO HER FATHER SURVIVE.

"I believe good philosophers, like eagles, fly alone, not in flocks like starlings."

In Rome, Galileo argued his ideas to anyone who listened. He was bold and confident. The ambassador from Tuscany grew alarmed for Galileo's safety. He "will get himself into trouble," the ambassador said, "for he is . . . stubborn and very worked up in this matter."

The Inquisition decided to meet and settle the issue once and for all. Galileo was not invited to present his ideas. In short order, the church banned Copernicus's theory, declaring it was "foolish and absurd." The Earth was the center of the universe.

The Inquisitors asked Cardinal Roberto Bellarmine to inform Galileo of the decision immediately. Bellarmine was known as the "hammer of the heretics." In 1600 he had helped sentence a heretic named Giordano Bruno to death. Bruno was burned alive at the stake.

Cardinal Bellarmine greeted Galileo with respect, his red cap in hand. But he grew stern as he spoke of the Inquisition's ruling. Galileo could no longer "hold or defend" the worldview of Copernicus. To do so "would be a very dangerous thing," said Bellarmine.

The air was knocked out of Galileo's big effort to sway the church. He returned home, silenced. For the next seven years, he heeded the Inquisition's warning and turned to other matters of science. Instead of gazing afar, he made himself a microscope and studied tiny insects up close. "I have observed many tiny animals with great admiration," he wrote, "among which the flea is quite horrible, the gnat and the moth very beautiful."

Then in 1623, exciting news arrived. Catholic cardinals had just elected a new pope, Urban VIII. Not only was he more open-minded about science, Pope Urban VIII was also a fan of Galileo. He had even written a poem praising the scientist.

It didn't take Galileo long to pay Pope Urban VIII a visit in Rome.

POPE URBAN VIII

# Chapter 8
## A Masterpiece

Galileo met with Pope Urban VIII six times during his visit to Rome in 1624. The two strolled through the Vatican Gardens, discussing astronomy. Galileo asked if the ban on Copernicus could be lifted.

Even though Urban had spoken out against the ban when he was a cardinal, he would not lift the ban now. The pope himself believed Aristotle's teachings. Nonetheless, he saw no harm in writing about Copernican theory for the sake of debate. He did give Galileo one strong caution, though: He must be careful to present the theory as an *unproven idea.*

Galileo returned home and eagerly took up his quill pen. He invented three characters who are friends. They meet over a four-day period to debate the hot topic: What stands at the center of the universe—the sun or the Earth? One friend, Sagredo, is the host who does not take sides in the argument. The second friend, named

Salviati, argues from the viewpoint of Copernicus. The third friend, Simplicio, defends Aristotle's belief. Surely, Galileo knew that the name *Simplicio* came very close to the Italian word for a simpleton—a fool!

Galileo wrote in Italian instead of Latin so common people could read the book. He made his arguments as easy to understand as possible. And in the margin, he supplied notes and drawings. His style was witty and highly readable. The final book was entitled *Dialogue Concerning the Two Chief World Systems.* It was a masterpiece—not just of science, but of literature, too.

Galileo finished writing in 1630. The *Dialogue* had taken him five years to write, because he was often sick. Now there was one last step. He had to send the book to the church censors in Rome for approval before it could be printed.

Then suddenly, the plague brought everything to a halt.

The plague was a deadly disease that had killed millions in Europe over hundreds of years. The outbreak of 1630 hit Tuscany. Panic set in. The plague spread quickly from one person to the next. The government sealed off the ill in their houses, hoping to contain the spread of the plague.

Galileo never became sick. However, he lost all contact with Rome. Roads were blocked to almost everyone. Finally, Rome sent word allowing churchmen in Florence to read his book, which was then approved.

In 1632 the *Dialogue* was finally published. As expected, the book delighted Galileo's friends . . . and outraged his enemies. Galileo thought he had played within the rules, debating both sides of the issue. But any reader could easily see which side he favored—that of Copernicus.

Pope Urban's reaction to the book was *not* expected. He switched sides, turning against Galileo! What had happened?

# THE PLAGUE

BEGINNING IN 1348, OUTBREAKS OF THE BUBONIC PLAGUE KILLED MILLIONS IN EUROPE. IT RAGED QUICKLY FROM VILLAGE TO VILLAGE, SPREAD BY RATS. VICTIMS DIED WITHIN A DAY OR TWO. PEOPLE CALLED IT THE BLACK DEATH BECAUSE OF THE WAY A VICTIM'S SKIN BLACKENED. FOR YEARS AT A TIME, THE PLAGUE WOULD DISAPPEAR, THEN RAGE AGAIN.

THE 1630 OUTBREAK IN FLORENCE SHUT DOWN THE CITY. NORMAL LIFE CAME TO A HALT. DOCTORS PROWLED THE STREETS, PICKING UP THE DEAD BODIES. THEY WORE STRANGE-LOOKING MASKS WITH BEAKS, STUFFED WITH STRAW AND HERBS, TO PROTECT THEM. BEFORE THE PLAGUE LEFT FLORENCE IN 1631, IT HAD TAKEN ABOUT ELEVEN THOUSAND LIVES OUT OF A POPULATION OF SEVENTY-FIVE THOUSAND PEOPLE.

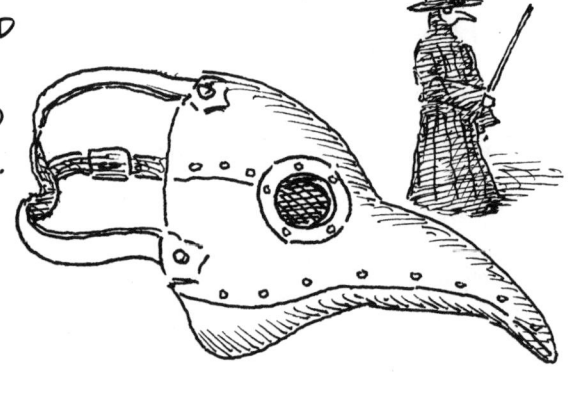

A religious war was raging in Europe between Catholics and Protestants. The pope was under pressure to take a hard line against anyone who challenged the church.

To make matters worse, Galileo's enemies told the pope that the *Dialogue* made fun of him. It put the pope's own words into the mouth of Simplicio, a fool!

Furious, Pope Urban ordered the Inquisition to investigate Galileo. It didn't take long for the church leaders to summon the scientist to Rome.

Why? To stand trial.

The charge: heresy.

Galileo's doctors pleaded that Galileo was too ill to travel. The Inquisition replied: Come willingly, or come in chains.

# Chapter 9
## On Trial

Galileo was seventy, an old man, when he arrived in Rome to stand trial. The pope could have jailed Galileo. Out of respect for his old age, however, he allowed Galileo to stay at the Medicis' embassy in Rome. The ambassador treated him as an honored guest.

The Inquisition did not. The court judges showed respect, but their questions were pointed and harsh. The trial would drag on for ten weeks. Galileo stood before the court on only four days, however.

Day one of questioning was April 12, 1633. The judges charged Galileo with writing a book that supported the ideas of Copernicus. Heresy! They claimed that Galileo had deliberately disobeyed church orders given to him back in 1616 on his earlier visit to Rome. The Inquisition had dug up their notes from that time. The notes stated that Galileo was warned not to "hold, teach, or defend" the Copernican system "*in any way whatsoever.*"

The notes rattled Galileo. Their warning went much further than anything he remembered Cardinal Bellarmine telling him in 1616. Galileo claimed strongly that he was innocent. In his own defense, he showed the judges a signed letter from Cardinal Bellarmine. It, too, was written in 1616. Galileo believed the letter said he could write about the Copernican system as a theory—a possibility. And he insisted that his book did just that.

The judges stuck by their own notes, however. By the end of the day, Galileo was deeply shaken. It was clear the Inquisition wanted to punish him.

Several days would pass before the second
hearing. Meanwhile, church officials met to review
the *Dialogue* again. Did it or did it not support
Copernicus? It most definitely did, they agreed.

Galileo "regards as mental dwarfs all who are not [followers of Copernicus]," one reviewer wrote. "It is clear enough what he has in mind."

On day two of questioning, Galileo stopped arguing his case and began to apologize. The extreme danger he faced had sunk in. He had done all in his power to convince the church of his views and his innocence, but to no avail. He was old, in poor health, and frightened. So Galileo admitted that his book had gone too far. Without meaning to, he had argued some points too forcefully in favor of Copernicus, he said.

On day three, the Inquisition pronounced Galileo's sentence: guilty! The judges told Galileo that he had brought upon himself "all the penalties" of heresy. In other words, he could be tortured and even put to death for his crime. But the judges allowed Galileo to escape the worst penalties if—and only if—he declared Copernicus wrong.

Galileo's spirit was crushed. He did not want to defy his church. Neither did he want to face torture.

On June 22, 1633, Galileo returned to court for the fourth and last time. He wore a long white robe, the sign of someone who regrets his sins.

Galileo fell to his knees. He began reading a statement that the court had prepared for him:

I, Galileo, son of the late Vincenzio Galilei of Florence, seventy years of age . . . abandon completely the false opinion that the Sun is at the center of the world and does not move and that the Earth is not the center and moves . . .

The Inquisition still punished Galileo so he would be "more cautious in the future and an example for others." His statement was to be publicly displayed in every university. His book, the *Dialogue,* was banned; all copies would be burned. Nor could Galileo publish any future books.

Then came the harshest punishment of all. Galileo was sentenced to house arrest for the rest of his life.

What must it have felt like for a scientist to lie about what he knew to be the truth? Yet more pain lay ahead for Galileo. His beloved daughter Maria Celeste died after a short illness, on April 2, 1634. She was just thirty-three years old. For weeks, Galileo could barely sleep or eat.

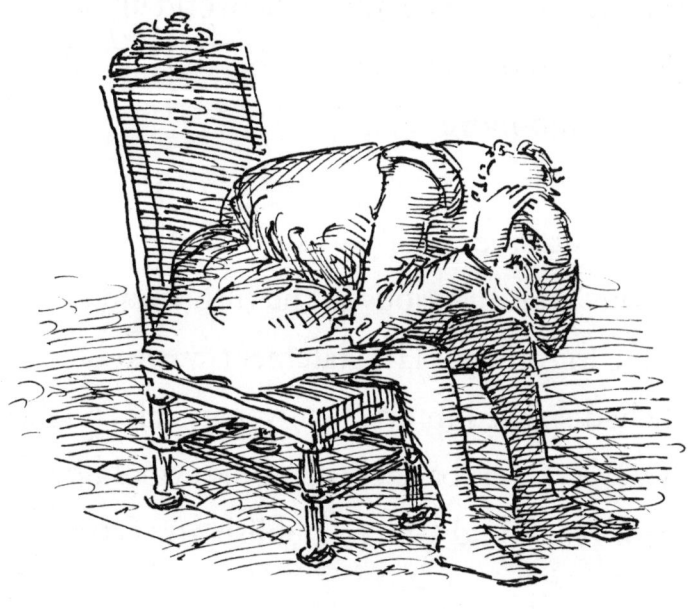

"I . . . continually hear my beloved daughter calling to me," he said. "She was a woman of exquisite mind, singular goodness, most tender in her feelings towards me."

# SUPPORTING GALILEO

DURING HIS WHOLE LIFE, GALILEO ENJOYED CLOSE TIES WITH HIGH-RANKING CATHOLICS, INCLUDING BISHOPS, ARCHBISHOPS, AND CARDINALS. SEVERAL OF THEM WERE WELL-KNOWN SCIENTISTS THEMSELVES. AT GALILEO'S TRIAL, THREE OF THE INQUISITION JUDGES DISAGREED WITH THE VERDICT AND REFUSED TO SIGN IT.

## Chapter 10
## Final Years

Galileo was locked inside his house at Arcetri for the last eight years of his life. He longed for the active social life he once led. He signed his letters, "from my prison." And he said he felt "stricken from the pages of life."

Yet his house stayed full with live-in guests. Pupils, along with Galileo's son, came to live with him and assist in his research. At one point, his sister-in-law moved in with four of her children! And sometimes, famous people visited from abroad —such as the poet John Milton from England.

What restored Galileo's spirit the most, perhaps, was getting back to work. Years earlier, he had studied motion. However, he had never gotten around to publishing his work.

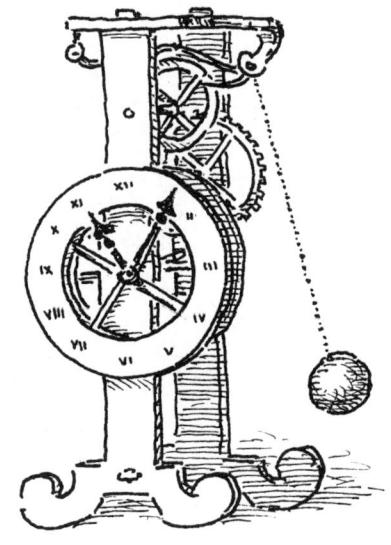

Now he returned to those experiments, adding to his discoveries. The old pendulum studies led him to invent a better clock. Until then, the best clocks were off by thirty minutes a day.

Galileo's last book, about the physics of motion and matter, was smuggled out of Italy and published in Holland in 1638. *Discourses Concerning Two New Sciences* laid new, important groundwork for future scientists. Fifty years later, the book inspired Isaac Newton to discover the law of gravity.

ISAAC NEWTON

In old age, Galileo became blind. Once he'd seen a shining new world through his telescope;

now he lived in darkness. Still, he kept working by dictating to his son and pupils.

Galileo died on January 8, 1642. He was seventy-eight years old.

His legacy lived on. Galileo's body of work made a huge impact on science. The modern physicist Albert Einstein named Galileo "the

father of modern physics—
indeed of modern science
altogether."

Galileo was a true
Renaissance man—a
man of many talents. He
was a mathematician,
a philosopher, and an
inventor. He excelled in the

ALBERT EINSTEIN

sciences of physics and astronomy. In addition,
he was an excellent writer
and artist.

POPE JOHN PAUL II

During the 1700s,
the sun-centered view of
the solar system slowly
became accepted. By
1835 the church lifted its
ban on works by Galileo
and Copernicus. And in
1992, Pope John Paul II

regretted the church's errors in regard to Galileo. Although the church had acted in good faith, the pope admitted that it had been wrong to turn astronomy into a matter of religion. This was just what Galileo had stated 350 years earlier.

History has heaped Galileo with praise. But perhaps the best tribute of all came from NASA—the US space agency. In 1989, NASA launched a spacecraft into outer space to study the planet Jupiter. The spacecraft's name? The *Galileo* orbiter!

# TIMELINE OF
# GALILEO'S LIFE

| | |
|---|---|
| 1564 | Galileo Galilei is born in Pisa, Italy, on February 15 |
| 1581 | Galileo enrolls at the University of Pisa |
| 1586 | Galileo invents a balance for weighing objects in air and water |
| 1589 | Galileo begins teaching mathematics at the University of Pisa |
| 1592 | The University of Padua hires Galileo to teach |
| 1597 | Galileo invents the geometric and military compass |
| 1599 | Galileo meets Marina Gamba, who will become the mother of his two daughters and son |
| 1604 | Galileo conducts important experiments on motion |
| 1610 | Galileo discovers the four moons of Jupiter *The Starry Messenger* is published Galileo is appointed mathematician and philosopher to the Grand Duke |
| 1616 | The Inquisition warns Galileo to stop defending the theory of Copernicus |
| 1630 | The plague invades Florence |
| 1632 | *Dialogue Concerning the Two Chief World Systems* is published |
| 1633 | The Inquisition sentences Galileo to house arrest |
| 1634 | Sister Maria Celeste, Galileo's older daughter, dies |
| 1638 | Galileo loses his eyesight |
| 1642 | Galileo dies on January 8 at home in Arcetri, Italy |

# TIMELINE OF THE WORLD

German Johannes Gutenberg invents the printing press — **1454**

Christopher Columbus arrives in the — **1492**
New World of the Americas

Portuguese explorer Vasco da Gama reaches India — **1498**

Ferdinand Magellan's crew finishes — **1522**
the first voyage around the world

Nicolaus Copernicus publishes his theory — **1543**
about a sun-centered universe

Artist Michelangelo dies in Rome, Italy, on February 18 — **1564**
Playwright and poet William Shakespeare is born
in England on April 23

Francis Drake sails around the world — **1577**
by way of Cape Horn

Jamestown is founded in North America — **1607**

Hans Lippershey invents the spyglass in Holland — **1608**

Builders complete the Taj Mahal in India — **1648**

Sir Isaac Newton publishes his theory — **1687**
of gravity in England

The Catholic Church lifts the ban on Galileo's works — **1835**

*Apollo 15* astronaut David Scott drops a hammer and — **1971**
feather on the moon to prove Galileo correct

NASA launches the *Galileo* spacecraft — **1989**
to study Jupiter

Pope John Paul II regrets the Church's mistakes — **1992**
regarding Galileo

# BIBLIOGRAPHY

* Doak, Robin S. **Galileo: Astronomer and Physicist**. Minneapolis: Compass Point Books, 2005.

**Galileo's Battle for the Heavens**. Writer and producer: David Axelrod. Director: Peter Jones. Nova Production/ WGBH, 2002.

MacLachlan, James. **Galileo Galilei: First Physicist**. New York: Oxford University Press, 1997.

* Mason, Paul. **Galileo**. Chicago: Heinemann, 2001.

* Panchyk, Richard. **Galileo for Kids: His Life and Ideas**. Chicago: Chicago Review Press, 2005.

Sobel, Dava. **Galileo's Daughter**. New York: Walker Publishing, 1999.


* Books for young readers

* Steele, Philip. **Galileo: The Genius Who Charted the Universe**. Washington, DC: National Geographic Society, 2005.

## WEBSITES

Galileo Legacy Site of NASA. http://galileo.jpl.nasa.gov/.

The Galileo Project of Rice University. http://galileo.rice.edu.